# THANK YOU

*for teaching me*

Teachers Name _____

Student Name _____

Class Name _____

Grade Level _____

Number Of Students _____

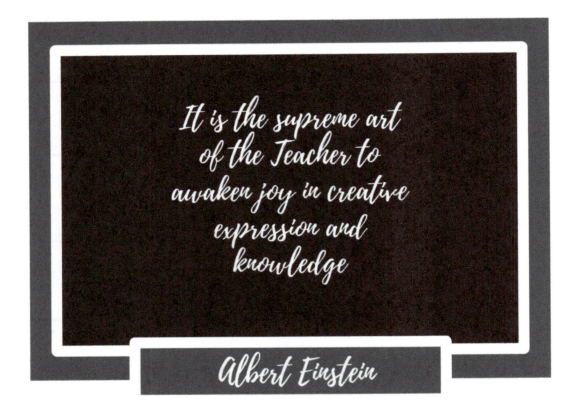

It is the supreme art of the Teacher to awaken joy in creative expression and knowledge

Albert Einstein

# Class Photo

I would like to say thank you for....

_____

_____

_____

_____

_____

_____

My Favorite memory......

_____

_____

_____

_____

_____

_____

Something I learned about you.........

_____

_____

_____

_____

_____

Something I learned about myself......

_____

_____

_____

_____

Our class loved it when.....

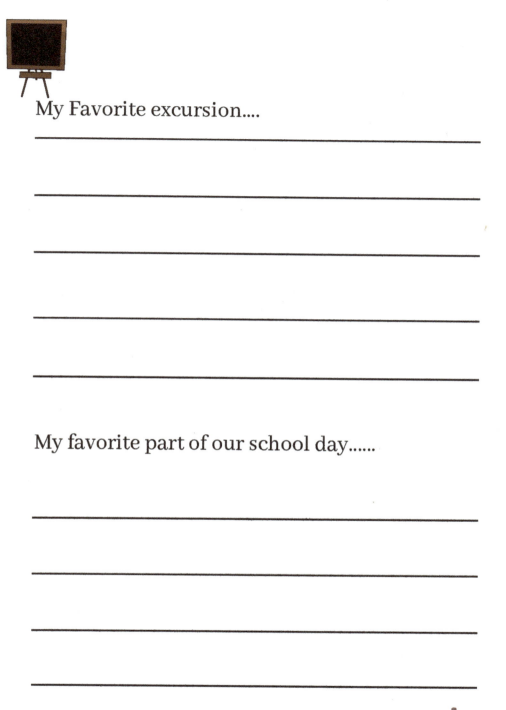

My Favorite excursion....

_____

_____

_____

_____

My favorite part of our school day......

_____

_____

_____

I have learned...............

_____

_____

_____

_____

Now I look forward to...........

_____

_____

_____

_____

My Favorite Day.......

_____

_____

_____

_____

_____

_____

_____

Things we made in class

My Favorite Artwork

The most challenging thing I did was.........

_____

_____

_____

_____

I appreciate you..........   THANK YOU

_____

_____

_____

I always looked forward to..........

_____

_____

_____

I would tell new students in your class next year......

# Drawing

I would like to say............

_____

_____

_____

_____

_____

_____

_____

_____

_____

_____

_____

A drawing of our classroom.....

I wish you a good holiday because..........

_____

_____

_____

_____

_____

_____

_____

_____

# Our School

It was funny when...............

_____

_____

_____

_____

Something that surprised me............

_____

_____

_____

_____

# Kindness

You taught me to .............

_____

_____

_____

_____

Something that I will never forget is.............

_____

_____

_____

_____

# Thank you

# My Teacher's Pages

My Favorite time of the School Day............

_____

_____

_____

Something I learned this year............

_____

_____

_____

 A class memory to Cherish...........

I will miss............

# Teacher Keepsakes

# One Hundred Years From Now

(excerpt from within my power by Forest Witcraft)

It will not matter
what kind of car I drove
what kind of house I lived in,
how much money was in my bank account
nor what my clothes looked like.
But the world may be a better place because
I was important in the life of a child

Lightning Source UK Ltd.
Milton Keynes UK
UKHW050747070720
366113UK00003B/65